It is impossible to keep a
straight face in the presence
of one or more kittens.

-Cynthia E. Varnado

In my head, the sky is blue, the grass
is green, and cats are orange.

—Jim Davis, In Dog Years I'd Be Dead: Garfield at 25

The only thing a cat worries about
is what's happening right now.

—Lloyd Alexander, Time Cat

Skiing Santa

The cat has too much spirit
to have no heart.

–*Ernest Menaul*

Santa's Helpers

Purrfect Holidays

The kitten was six weeks old.
It was enchanting, a delicate
fairy-tale cat.

—Doris Lessing, On Cats

_____
_____
_____
_____
_____
_____
_____
_____

Purrfect Holidays

All the world is happy when
Santa Claus comes.

–Maud Lindsay

_____

_____

_____

_____

_____

_____

_____

_____

_____

_____

Let us have music for Christmas...
Sound the trumpet of
joy and rebirth;
Let each of us try, with a
song in our hearts,
To bring peace to men on earth.

–Mildred L. Jarrell

Candy Snow

'Tis the season to be aware of
the tiny magic everywhere.

–Unknown

Cats are cats...the world over! These intelligent, peace-loving, four-footed friends—who are without prejudice, without hate, without greed—may someday teach us something.

–Lilian Jackson Braun, *The Cat Who Had 60 Whiskers*

At Christmas, all roads lead home.

–Marjorie Holmes

A Christmas candle is a lovely thing;
It makes no noise at all,
But softly gives itself away;
While quite unselfish, it grows small.

-Eva K. Logue

_____
_____
_____
_____
_____
_____
_____
_____

Dream Candle

Snow provokes responses that
reach right back to childhood.

—Andy Goldsworthy

Making a Friend

He was dressed all in fur, from his
head to his foot, and his clothes were
all tarnished with ashes and soot.
A bundle of toys he had flung on his back,
and he looked like a peddler
just opening his pack.

-Clement Clarke Moore

Santa's Bag

What fun to be a cat!

-Christopher Morley

_____
_____
_____
_____
_____
_____
_____
_____
_____
_____

Christmas Lights

There are few things in life more
heartwarming than to be
welcomed by a cat.

–Tay Hohoff

_____
_____
_____
_____
_____
_____
_____
_____
_____
_____

Kittens at the Window

Christmas is most truly Christmas when
we celebrate it by giving
the light of love to those
who need it most.

–Ruth Carter Stapleton

_____
_____
_____
_____
_____
_____
_____
_____
_____
_____

It is a very inconvenient habit of kittens
(Alice had once made the remark)
that whatever you say
to them, they always purr.

–Lewis Carroll, Through the Looking Glass

Ho Ho Ho

Cats never listen.
They're dependable that way.

–Seanan McGuire, *Rosemary and Rue*

Christmas without elves
isn't a Christmas at all.

–Unknown

Gingerbread Sleigh

© Kayomi Harai • From *Santa's Kitty Helpers Holiday Coloring Book* • © Design Originals, www.D-Originals.com

Never try to outstubborn a cat.

-Robert A. Heinlein

_____

_____

_____

_____

_____

_____

_____

_____

_____

Bell Stocking

Blessed is the season which
engages the whole world in
a conspiracy of love!

–Hamilton Wright Mabie

Noel Angel

The cat has always been associated with the moon.
Like the moon it comes to life at night, escaping from
humanity and wandering over housetops with its eyes
beaming out through the darkness.

–Patricia Dale Green

_____
_____
_____
_____
_____
_____
_____
_____
_____
_____

Santa on the Moon

My idea of Christmas,
whether old-fashioned or modern,
is very simple: loving others.

–Bob Hope

_____
_____
_____
_____
_____
_____
_____
_____
_____
_____

Christmas Mailbox

Cats do not have to be shown how to
have a good time, for they are unfailing
ingenious in that respect.

–James Mason

We elves try to stick to the four main
food groups: candy, candy canes,
candy corns, and syrup.

-Elf

Perhaps the best Yuletide decoration
is being wreathed in smiles.

–Unknown

Happy Wreath

At Christmas, play and
make good cheer,
for Christmas comes
but once a year.

–Thomas Tusser

Holiday Joy

A kitten is, in the animal world,
what a rosebud is in the garden.

-Robert Southey

Meowy Christmas!

Peace On Earth

Heap on the wood!
The wind is chill;
But let it whistle as it will,
We'll keep our Christmas merry still.

–Sir Walter Scott

Peace on Earth

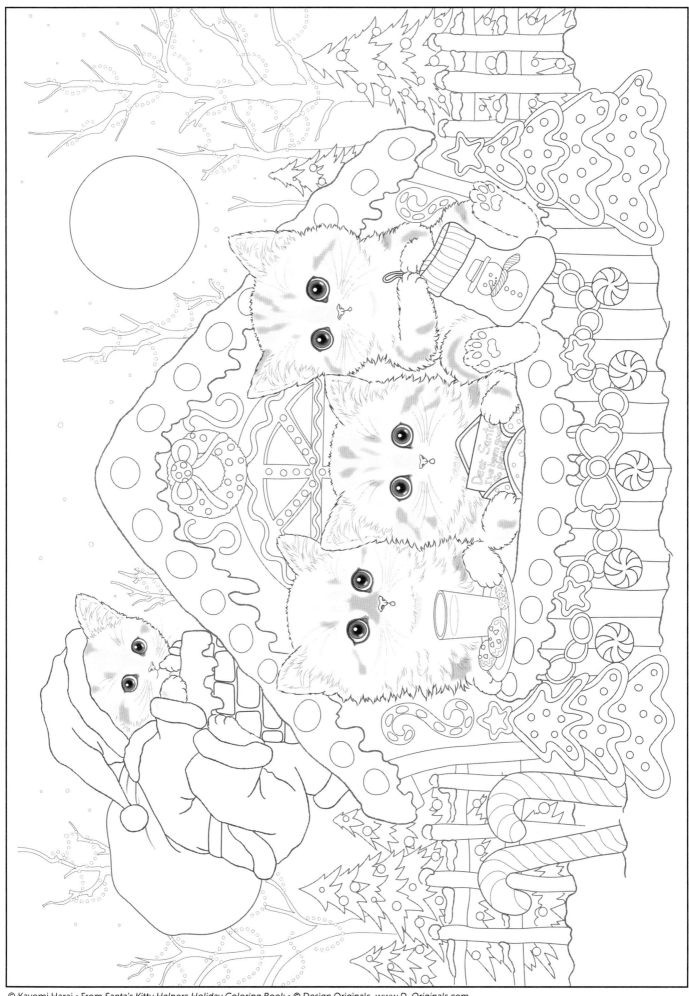

I love cats because I enjoy my home;
and little by little, they become
its visible soul.

—Jean Cocteau

_____
_____
_____
_____
_____
_____
_____
_____

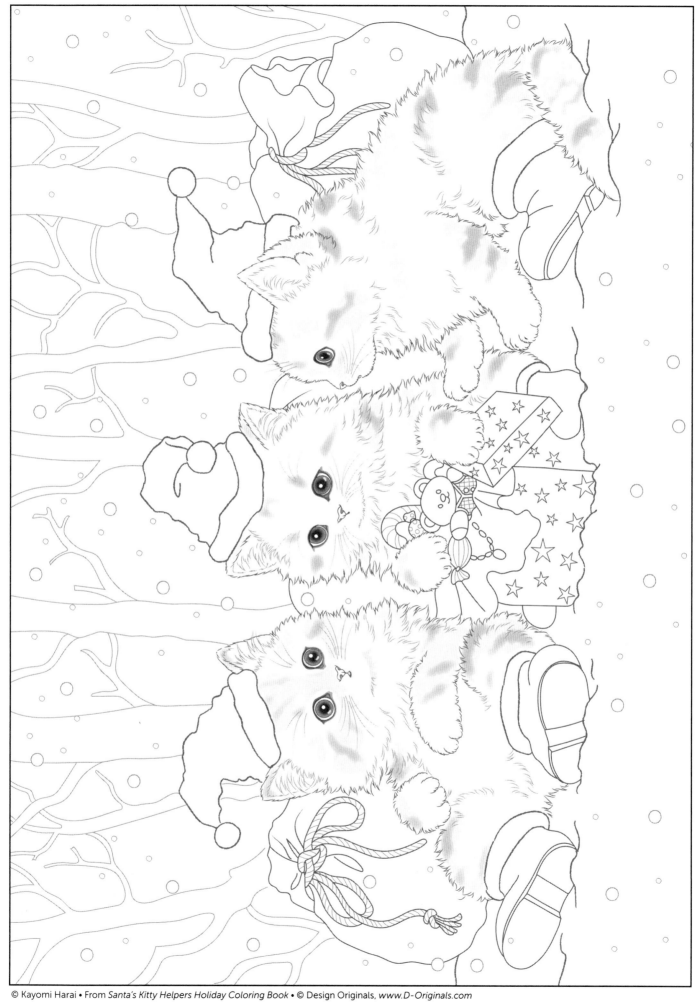

One kind word can warm
three winter months.

—Japanese proverb

_____
_____
_____
_____
_____
_____
_____
_____
_____
_____

Kitty Boots

They err who think Santa Claus
enters through the chimney.
He enters through the heart.

-Charles W. Howard